Window Dressing

Homes & Ideas
Window Dressing

Annie Ashworth

BOXTREE

Welcome to the *Homes & Ideas* book of *Window Dressing*. *Homes & Ideas* is the magazine for bright, creative and budget-conscious home style, and is absolutely packed with informative and inspiring ideas. Lifestyles and homes are constantly changing, and with them are the needs of our readers. More ideas, more information and more easy-to-follow projects are always in demand, and it was this demand which has prompted the idea of a series of books covering in greater detail the most popular topics featured in *Homes & Ideas*. *Window Dressing* includes lots of inspirational ideas – whatever the type of room. It tackles everyday problems – how to deal with doorways, archways and huge bow windows, and includes pages of creative projects from easy-to-make Roman blinds to classic French pleating. It is a perfect partner for *Homes & Ideas* and will provide you with all the answers to the most popular questions regarding the best window dressings for your home.

Debbie Djordjevic
Editor – *Homes & Ideas*

Contents

Introduction

If windows are our view out onto the world (and everybody else's view in), then the last thing they should be is boring.

In fact, windows come in such a great variety of shapes and sizes, and can be dressed in so many different ways, that window dressing is a marvellous excuse to be as theatrical and flamboyant, as simple and modern, or as whimsical and romantic as you feel. There are no hard and fast rules about which style should go where, nor are there restrictions of fashion. And there is no need to be restrained by the practicalities, such as the need to block out a draught or hide an ugly view, or, least of all, a tight budget. Window dressing need not be expensive. Effective and appealing curtains and blinds can be made from virtually any material.

This book will help you to transform even the most awkwardly shaped windows, showing you some of the huge variety of styles, from heavy flounces to floaty voiles, and giving easy-to-follow, step-by-step guidelines to help you recreate each look. There's a chapter on blinds and pelmets, with full instructions for making them, and finally there are ideas for those all-important finishing touches, the little details which make the difference between the mundane and the magnificent.

1 Ideas and inspiration

Windows need to be flexible. They need to let in light and fresh air, and they need to block out the cold. The way you dress your windows needs to pay equal attention to practicalities as to good looks. Whether you are dressing just one window, or all the windows in a new home, you need to ask yourself a few questions.

1. Do you need to block out a draught?

If so, you must consider a thick covering, probably curtains rather than blinds, using a warm, closely woven fabric, with thermal linings. The pole should be sufficiently close to the frame to avoid letting cold air in around it.

2. Is there a dreary view to hide?

Not everyone is lucky enough to have a beautiful view from every window. You could make the window the centre of attention by draping a curtain across it, or hanging an interesting blind with trimmings (both options will block out a certain amount of light). A classy version of the net curtain provides a good answer. Pretty lace or thin muslin will let in light, whilst completely obscuring the view, more so if the fabric is hung flat. Venetian blinds give the option of letting in light or shutting it out.

Why not dispense with a curtain or blind altogether? A pot plant, or pretty glass or *objets d'art* placed on shelves set into the window are interesting and distracting. You might like to hang stained-glass plaques, or use stained panels to create interesting light patterns.

3. Do you want to draw attention to a beautiful view or window?

In this case, allow the curtain to frame the window like a picture. Choose a fabric which reflects the colours of the view behind: greens and blues towards the sea, natural colours for trees. Use the colours in the view as if they were a colour card, and find the complementary colours to highlight them. Again, you may choose to dispense with curtains (**above right**). If practicalities such as draught exclusion can be dispensed with, frame the window with a fabulous pelmet or lambrequin (see Chapter 3). These work like a picture frame, leading the eye to the image beyond.

4. Do you want privacy?

Blinds are the obvious answer **(right)**, especially Venetian ones, though, even if they are plain white, blinds will block out light to some extent. Etched glass will obscure the view whilst making the most of the light, and works well in a bathroom. The light will make pretty patterns where it falls.

5. Will the room be used at a particular time of day?

This has a very important influence on the type of fabric or window dressing style. A sitting room used only in the evening can afford to have curtains in heavier fabric and richer colours, which reflect lamp light well, are cosy and provide good insulation in the winter. A bedroom, especially one with an east facing window, might demand thinner curtains which will filter early morning light, but fill the room with a positive colour at the beginning of the day.

6. Are there lots of differently shaped windows in the room?

It is usually best to treat groups of windows with identical curtains or blinds, and where there is a door between two windows, to cover all three with a blind **(above)**. This will help to prevent a busy, cluttered effect. If all the other windows are to be curtained, and one shape remains difficult to treat in the same way, cover it with a blind in the same fabric so that it blends in.

7. Do you want to follow a particular fashion/ style around the house and/or be true to the house's period?

If so, this may make it easier to find window dressing solutions, though practicalities will dictate to a certain extent. You may not be able to have heavy Victorian-style drapes in the bathroom, but a single *faux* curtain pulled to the side by a tassel, with a practical blind to let down for privacy would work just as well (see Chapter 3 for ideas on this theme). In fact, a variety of styles around the house (though not in the same room) can make for more interesting surroundings.

8. Do you need to block out light?

A complete blackout will prevent children waking too early in the summer months. Use blackout lining on curtains, or hang a blackout roller blind with a pretty, more opaque curtain in front (choose a fabric to match the room's colour scheme).

Strong sunlight shining into a south facing room can fade delicate fabrics. Protect them by hanging, behind the room drapes, a gauze curtain or blind which can be pulled back when the light is dull (for suitable track see page 60).

9. What are the practical considerations?

Once you have considered all the above questions, and before you make your final decision on style and fabric, think hard about the following practicalities:

• Will your choice of fabric keep the room warm/cool enough?

• Will there be a lot of moisture in the room (kitchen/bathroom) which might affect the fabric?

• Will the curtains get dirty by the very nature of where they are to hang (by a doorway, or in a child's room), and is the fabric machine-washable? Full, trailing curtains on hard flooring in an area of busy traffic will soon have dirty hems.

• Will the chosen style of curtain or blind cope if it will be opened and shut very often? Roman or Austrian blinds are more fiddly than roller blinds, and curtains with drawstrings are smoother in action and become less grubby than curtains on a traditional pole.

If curtains might be splashed, would a roll-up blind be a better solution? At least make sure the curtains can be tied right back.

12

RULES OF WINDOW DRESSING

• Make the view beyond a window an integral part of the whole look, whether you want to make the most of it, or obscure it completely.

• Choose the style of pole, finial and tieback when choosing your fabric, not as an afterthought.

• When measuring up for classic gathered curtains, never skimp on the width, otherwise they will look mean. If you need to economize, choose a simpler style of curtain and heading.

• Bold patterns and colours look better on ungathered headings like tabs, ties or hooks, and involve less fabric to make them up.

• Allow for the shrinkage that will occur when curtain or blind fabric is cleaned for the first time.

• In general, curtains that are to hang full length in straight folds need heavy fabric. Heavy fabric works best with tailored, pleated headings. Loose gathers and ties work better with lightweight fabrics.

• Avoid using precious fabric for lining, as this is the most likely part of the curtain to fade.

• If you are planning curtains which fall in folds on the floor, consider the floor surface, and how dirty the curtain fabric will become. Carpet or matting would be better than hard flooring.

• Austrian blinds are designed for tall windows and look foolish covering a small window.

Awkward windows: easy solutions

Beautifully shaped arched windows can be hard to deal with. Hang curtains from high above the arch, falling right to the floor, and make sure the pole or curtain track is wide enough so that the curtains can be pulled right back to show the whole window. If you choose to hang a blind, make sure it too is hung high above the arch of the window. Curved curtain track can be run round the arch, with curtains or an Austrian blind hung in gathers, emphasising the shape of the arch.

Above: **Where a window sits right against a wall or wardrobe, fix the heading to both ends of the pole or track and hook the curtain back with a tieback.**
Left: **Skylight windows often look good left uncovered to let in a generous flood of light. In a bedroom, fix the top of the curtain above the window on a pole, and hold the curtain back with a second pole beneath the window. Alternatively, attach headings to both the top and bottom of the curtain and fix to tracks above and beneath the window, or use roller blinds (adding a cleat to secure the cord).**

Leave skylights above a doorway uncovered, and add a curtain on a simple pole over the doorway for privacy.

Above: **Quirky windows like this round one are often best left well alone to create a centre of attention. Windows that do not need curtains or blinds for warmth or privacy can look very effective with shelves set into the recess. These can provide a home for colourful glass bottles or could be hung with crystals or strings of glass beads which catch the light, making more of a northern prospect or an uninspiring view.**

Left: **For a deeply recessed window, hang a blind in the recess or hang a curtain right across the front of the recess, especially if the window opens inwards. Here, fabric has been looped loosely over the pole for a luxurious look, and pictures have been hung on the wall of the recess.**

For difficult dormer windows, use dormer rods, fixed to the top corners of the window frame. The curtains are gathered onto hooks on the rod itself, and can be fixed back in daytime to allow in the maximum amount of light. Use your main fabric for both the curtain and the lining, or use contrasting lining. Let the curtains hang just to the sill.

Looking for fabrics and avoiding mistakes

The number of fabrics available these days is almost overwhelming, and interior design shops have row upon row of sample books. If you have considered the points at the beginning of this chapter, you should have a good idea of what you want, or at least what you don't want. You probably won't be looking for heavy velvets for a bathroom, nor chintz for a modern dining room, and these sorts of decisions will have helped to narrow the field. Have some idea too of design, whether it be abstract, floral, striped, textured and so on. Your budget will have narrowed the field even further. Once you have a rough idea about the thickness, length, and required characteristics of the fabric, you can focus on finding fabrics that will fit the bill.

Don't be afraid to ask for advice. Salespeople in specialist shops/departments have a good idea of which fabrics will work with which type of heading, so check with them the width and cleaning requirements of the fabric. You are usually allowed to borrow samples and sample books for a small deposit (even free sometimes) to take home, and it is often worth ordering a larger sample of fabric (usually free) to make absolutely sure you have made the right decision. Before finally ordering your fabric, choose the lining, trimmings, tiebacks, etc. When your fabric is being measured out, or when you go to collect ordered fabric, check that there are no imperfections and that it has been cut from the same roll. Colour can vary dramatically from roll to roll.

Although bay windows are an attractive shape, they can be a challenge to dress. The traditional solution is a shaped track with a running pelmet along all three sides and a pair of curtains for each window, but these wooden shutters, with their faintly colonial look, are both practical and a little more unusual.

2 Making curtains

Once you have an idea of the practical requirements of your curtains, the question of the type of heading will probably answer itself. The fabric you have chosen and its weight will dictate what sort of heading is necessary, whether the fabric needs to be lined, and whether it will sit better on a track or a pole. Certain headings will result in a full curtain, others give a tailored look; some are so elegant or unusual, they are a feature in themselves.

Though the professional method is to hand sew curtain headings (see page 26), for most styles, special stiffened heading tape, available in different weights and widths, will do the job very well. Use these heading tapes on thicker, lined curtains. For unlined or sheer curtains, though tapes can be used, often loops or decorative hooks will do the trick.

Although there are many styles of heading to choose from, there are six classic treatments. If you can orchestrate a little space to work in, curtains are very simple to make at home, and once you have mastered the classics, then you will be able to take on bigger challenges later.

CHECKLIST FOR MAKING CURTAINS

• Always measure up for a curtain with the track or pole in place. Use a retractable metal tape measure.

• Check measurements twice so you are absolutely sure they are correct, and remember to include seam and hem allowances.

• Measure both sides of the window, as floors can be uneven.

• Allow for any pattern repeat on the fabric, that is the length of one complete pattern, in order to match the pattern across the curtains. Work out how many repeats you will need to cut to fit the drop (the length of curtain) required. There may well be some wastage, especially with fabrics which have large repeats – some can be as much as half the drop of the curtain.

• If a radiator is positioned behind the curtain, allow plenty of space between the top of the curtain and the wall to allow the air to circulate, or hang curtains to the length of the window sill.

• Make sure you have all your trimmings, lining and interlining and enough of the right coloured thread before you start making the curtains.

• Find a clean, clear work area, with plenty of good light, ideally where you can leave your work out.

• Keep an ironing board close to hand for pressing seams, lining, etc.

Loose blind curtains with a gathered heading, held back with simple tiebacks are the easiest type for the beginner to tackle. A plywood pelmet painted in a co-ordinated colour and running right across the wall solves a difficult window dressing problem.

Measuring up

1. Decide on the length of the curtains you require. Position the track or pole just above the window, fixed to the wall or architrave. For sill-length curtains, measure – using a metal rule – from the top of the curtain track (or the eyes on the rings of a curtain pole) to 5mm above the sill and add a hem allowance. For floor-length curtains, measure to a point 1cm above the floor to allow for clearance, then add a hem allowance. For floor-draped curtains, measure to the floor then add 5-10cm and a hem allowance. Add hem and heading measurements to the total drop, plus any extra for pattern repeat (always check the curtain-making instructions for the recommended hem allowance; for example, sheer cotton curtains will require a smaller hem allowance than heavier fabrics). You may also need to allow for headings that stand up above the track.

2. When calculating the length of the track or pole, allow space for pulling the curtain back in the daytime. Heavy, interlined fabrics need more space than light-weight curtains. For the width of fabric for each curtain, measure the length of the track or pelmet board, or from the first ring on each end of a pole (this is where the pole is attached to the wall), and multiply this by the required fullness for your chosen heading. (For example, to make a gathered head, the flat, ungathered width should be two and a half times the finished width. For a curtain with an unpleated heading, the flat curtain should be one and a half times the finished width.) Add side turnings as recommended in the instructions.

3. Once you have measured the track or pole and decided on the fullness and length you require you can calculate the amount of fabric you need, which depends on how many widths (drops) are needed for each curtain.

Fabric comes in widths of 120-150cm. For example: you have chosen unpatterned fabric which is 137cm wide, and the curtain length is to be 180cm. A pair of curtains which needs two widths of fabric in each cur-

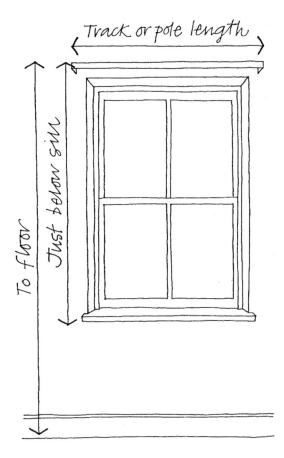

Track or pole length

Just below sill

To floor

tain will need four drops in total. Therefore, you need 180cm x 4, which equals 7.2m of fabric, plus the recommended hem and heading allowance x 4.

A pair of curtains the same length with only one width per curtain (tab-headed curtains, for example) will need only two drops of fabric or 3.6m plus hem and heading allowance. A pair with one-and-a-half widths per curtain will need three drops or 5.4m plus hem and heading allowance.

4. Patterned fabric will have a pattern repeat. Add the length of the repeat to each drop. To check the repeat, match the pattern across the finished curtain, with a complete motif at the top of each drop. When made up, both curtains should match in this way.

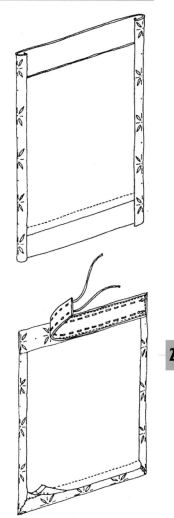

Making lined curtains

A loose-lined curtain is the easiest type to make. The process is straightforward, and important to master before trying more complicated projects. These instructions are for a simple gathered heading.

You will need:

- Fabric
- Lining or contrasting fabric (lining fabric should be 23cm shorter and 12.5cm narrower than the main fabric)
- Weights (optional but they make a curtain hang better)
- Heading tape

Note: When you have cut the fabric, check that the pieces are all lying on a straight horizontal grain, by pulling out one thread across the top of each drop.

1. Join widths of curtain fabric if necessary, using flat seams (see page 62) and matching any pattern. Press the seams open and repeat the process for the lining.

2. Turn up 2.5cm to the wrong side of the lining twice to create a double hem. With a pin mark the mid-points of the curtain panels and lining panels.

3. Place the lining and the fabric right sides together, with the lining 7.5cm down from the top, and align the side edges. The main fabric will be fuller than the lining. Pin

and tack, then machine stitch 1cm seams, stopping 2.5cm from the bottom hemmed edge of the lining.

4. Turn the curtain right side out and press, matching the mid-points of curtain and lining panels to make equal margins of curtain fabric on each side.

5. Press a 7.5cm double hem (making it 15cm in total) on the curtain fabric. The lining should finish 5cm above the finished bottom of the curtain.

6. Mitre the corners following the technique outlined on page 62.

7. To weight the curtain, sew weighted tape into the base of the hem. Alternatively, insert disc weights at regular intervals. Slipstitch the hem.

8. Turn down the 7.5cm at the top edge of the curtain (so that it meets the top of the lining), angling it slightly at each corner. Attach the heading tape to cover the raw edge. Knot the cords at one end of the tape, leaving the other end free. Machine stitch the tape along the sides and ends, turning the ends under but not sewing over the free cords. Both lines of sewing should be in the same direction to prevent puckering.

9. Pull the cords gently to gather the curtain to the required width. Knot the ends into a bow; alternatively use a cord tidy. Do not cut off any cord because you will need to pull the curtains flat again when they are washed or dry cleaned.

10. Insert the required number of hooks into the heading tape, spacing them evenly, and hang the curtain onto the track or pole.

26

Gathered heading

Narrow gathers are most suitable when the curtain will be hidden beneath a pelmet or flounce. Even heavy fabric can be gathered onto heading of a suitable weight, and the fabric will fall in a soft, informal look. The gathered heading is then hooked onto a double pelmet track, which also holds the pelmet. The pelmet can be as informal or tailored as you choose.

Gathers can also look very effective on lighter weight curtains, as on this door **(above left)**. The fabric has been gathered onto a cased heading, and threaded over a decorative dormer rod, the stand-up frill at the top of the curtain making an attractive detail.

HAND-SEWN CURTAINS

These days there is a sew-on tape for virtually every type of curtain heading which makes life a great deal easier – especially for the amateur curtain maker. Purists would argue, however, that the only way to make curtains properly is to use sew-on or iron-on curtain buckram on the heading, and to sew on webbing and curtain hooks. This method does do away with rows of machine stitches, but it is more complicated. In addition curtain buckram does soften somewhat when it is cleaned. You will have to decide which method suits you – but hand sewing is really only recommended for professional makers or true perfectionists.

Pleated heading

Pencil pleats (a row of evenly spaced deep pleats) or triple pleats (pleats grouped in threes) create a more formal look, and the fabric on a deep, pleated heading falls straight in full, tailored folds. This style looks marvellous on a grander window, perhaps in a drawing room or on a landing, where the curtains can fall right to the floor and where a patterned fabric will be seen clearly. It is a strong enough heading style for heavier fabrics which are also interlined, but will look very good with most fabrics, anywhere.

Both styles can be made with commercial heading tape, following the basic method for lined curtains. Pencil and triple pleats need about two-and-a-half times more fabric than the width of pleated curtain required, depending on the make of heading tape used. Allow 15cm between pleats, and space them evenly, or symmetrically in the case of triple pleats. Heading tape for double pleats is available, and special triple pleat heading tape makes the gathering much easier.

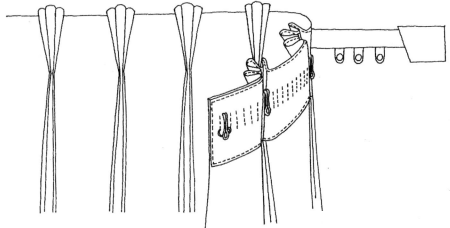

Tab heading

This heading style only works on a pole, but dispenses with the need for rings or hooks. The tabs simply loop over the pole, attached to the back of a pleated, unpleated, gathered, stiffened or unstiffened heading, though it perhaps looks best on a simple ungathered, unlined curtain in good-quality cotton. These curtains have an informality which really suits a child's room.

1. Each curtain should be one and a half times the width of half the window (or two thirds the width of the whole window) so that it falls in very gentle gathers. Allow 9cm for both hem and heading, and 4cm for side seams. Make up each curtain, turning in 1cm double seams (2cm in all) and a 2.5cm double hem at the bottom of each curtain (5cm in all).

2. You will need a tab about every 10cm along the finished (gathered) width of the curtain. Measure around the pole to calculate the length needed for the tabs. This will depend on the width of the pole, but keep your measurements generous so that the tabs are not tight making the curtain difficult to close. Allow 2cm on the tab length for stitching the tabs onto the heading. The width of the tabs must be twice the finished width, plus two seam allowances.

3. Fold each strip in half lengthways, right sides together, and stitch along the sides and at one end.

4. Turn the tabs right side out (you may need to insert a pointed object like a knitting needle to push out the points of each tab), and press. Neatly tuck in the raw edge at the open end of each tab and stitch up, then fold each strip in half to make a loop.

5. Fold a double 1cm turning (2cm in all) at the top of the curtain fabric and tack. Now position the tabs, tacking them into place, one at each end of the curtain then at regular intervals along the back of the heading. Machine stitch into place along the whole width of each curtain with two lines of stitching. Slot the pole through the tabs.

Note: For a tied heading, make up the curtain and the tabs as above, making twice as many tabs. Each tab should be long enough to form half of a bow

Goblet heading

This is a very elegant heading style which lends itself particularly well to a curved pelmet board, and a fixed heading (see page 20). A goblet heading looks excellent dressed up with details like tassels or cording, even covered buttons sewn on at the base of each goblet.

1. Make up a curtain using special goblet heading tape pushing out the upper sections of the pleat into a cup shape.

2. Fill the cup with wadding or folded interlining to keep it plump.

3. To add cord and tassel detail, loop the cord, pining it to every third or fourth goblet, depending on the width of the curtain. Stitch into place picking up only a few threads from the front of the curtain, and let the tassels at each end hang down in equal lengths.

when tied over the pole. Position the tabs in pairs at intervals as above. Stitch in place using two lines of machine stitching. Hang the curtain by tying the tabs in bows over the pole.

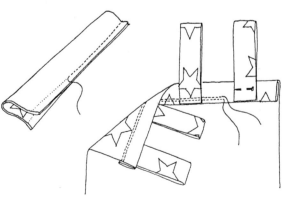

TIP

To ensure that headings run smoothly over poles, take down the curtains and spray the poles with furniture polish, buffing with a clean duster.

Eyelet heading

Eyelets are a rather unusual treatment, which would suit a contemporary fabric in a modern setting. Make up a pair of lined or unlined curtains, the ungathered width only slightly wider than half the window to give a gentle gather. Finish off the top with a small turn, then insert eyelets using an eyelet tool, available from haberdashers. Hang the curtains using generously sized split hooks, or seek out more unusual hooks like these ones **(right)**, which are based on butcher's hooks.

Another idea is to pierce a plain stiffened heading with large eyelets then insert a metal rod or curtain wire

through the eyelets. This works well for a run of tall windows **(above)**, and is economical because you need less fullness than in a conventional curtain. It is also an excellent means of curtaining off an area of a room.

No-sew curtains

The easiest curtains in the world are economical with fabric, with your time and with trimmings. This unlined cotton **(below)** is only one fabric width wide. (You may have to stitch a small hem around each edge to stop fraying.) These curtains are hung from the pole using neat (and very cheap) clip-on curtain hooks, though pin-on hooks would work just as well. Muslin or thin cotton with an appliqué pattern looks stunning in a bedroom, billowing in front of an open window with the early morning sun shining through. Calico would also be a good choice and could be cut with pinking shears.

Felt too is ideal for no-sew curtains because the fabric does not fray, is a good insulator, and comes in deep jewel-like colours. A bold blanket stitch along the edges in a strong dark colour would add interest.

31

TIP

Plastic curtain hooks are adequate for hanging nets, unlined and simple lined curtains, but brass hooks are best for heavier, interlined curtains. A 2.5cm heading tape only has one hook pocket, whereas the wider tapes will have a choice of two or three, so you can vary the length of the curtains. For uncorded tapes use metal pin hooks.

3 Tiebacks, pelmets and trimmings

A window dressing project is best planned as a complete concept, including accessories. The small details can really make a difference, doing justice to expensive fabric, dressing up cheap fabric, helping to frame a view, and, especially with imaginatively-shaped pelmets, helping to make an interesting window fascinating.

Try to imagine how your curtains will look when they are hung and think about other details in the room – the style of furniture, mantelpiece, wallpaper, and any picture rail or cornice. These details may help you to decide whether your window dressing could have a colonial feel (if the floors are wooden, and the windows sash), a rather grand look (high ceilings and enough space for you to be theatrical with flounces and swags) or a cottage style (where gathered pleats and more simple lines would feel more at home). Then you will be able to choose from a long list of possibilities.

Tiebacks

The poor old tieback has been much maligned, and justifiably so. Too often it is a mean little device which hangs limply around thin curtains to no real effect. The true role of the tieback is to scoop back a curtain, making the most of its fullness. The tieback should shape a window by creating a soft, gentle line, and

Left: **A rigid arm, protruding from the wall on each side of the window, is the simplest device for holding back curtains. It can be wooden or brass, decorative or plain, and is fixed to the wall by slotting it into a cup which is itself screwed into the wall.** Right: **This novel idea is a large-link chain (cut to length from hardware shops) and held back with a metal hook.**

You will need:
- Main fabric
- Lining
- Interlining
- Interfacing
- Paper for a template
- Bias binding or trimming (optional)
- Hook and curtain rings

1. Measure loosely around the curtain at the height you want the tieback to be, to the point where it will hook onto the wall.

2. Cut out the shape you require for the tieback from a piece of paper, then use the template to cut out the shape in lining interfacing and interlining, then again in main fabric, adding a 2.5cm seam allowance on this measurement.

3. Place the interlining on the interfacing, then stretch the main fabric around both, cutting and trimming the excess. Press the turnings with a hot iron to fuse them to the interfacing.

4. Cut and glue on (using fabric glue) any bias strip or trimming around the edges of the tieback.

5. Place the lining over the back of the tieback, fold in the edges, and slipstitch into position. Press with a hot iron to release the interfacing glue.

6. Stitch rings to the inside of the tieback at both ends, and attach a hook to the wall at the required height.

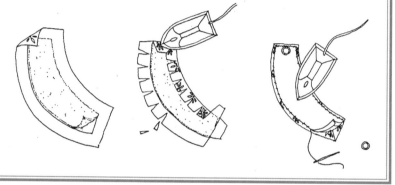

should even be a fabulous detail in itself. The only rules which apply to tiebacks are as follows:

• They must be the right proportion in relation to the curtain, so that they do not look foolish or 'disappear'. They must be long enough to hug, not strangle, the curtain.

• You must be disciplined enough to tie them back each

A stiffened piece of fabric that contrasts with or matches the curtain fabric is the most familiar tieback style. The cross stitch on this tieback makes an effective contrast with the plain curtain.

morning, arranging the curtains attractively. If you are busy or lazy by nature, then a brass or wooden arm device over which you simply hang the curtain may be the answer!

• The fixings must be securely attached to the wall. A loose tieback is useless.

Decorative tiebacks are features in themselves. Painted shells, plump velvet or paper flowers, or fruit sewn onto a plain fabric tieback look stunning, as would arrangements of dried flowers or large buttons and bows. The tieback on page 32 is decorated with velvet hearts filled with lavender for a fragrant welcome. However, the sheer intricacy of these styles means they are really best suited to a single curtain which is permanently pulled back, perhaps over a doorway, or at a window which also has a roller or roman blind.

Tieback devices can be inexpensive and very simple. The most popular easy option is one of the many ready-made tassel and cord tiebacks. Look out too for beads in colours which co-ordinate with the curtains and which can be strung like a necklace onto cord and hooked over tieback hooks (a tassel would finish them off with a flourish).

Plaited tiebacks look very effective when made in three fabrics which contrast with the main curtain

fabric. Measure up for the tieback (see page 34), and make three tubes of fabric as follows:

• Cut a width of fabric for each tube to twice the width of the finished tube, plus a seam allowance.

• Fold the fabric in half lengthways, right sides together, and pin, tack and stitch. Press the seam so that it runs along the centre of the tube. Stitch across one end of the tube, and turn right side out.

• Cut a narrow length of wadding to fit inside the tube and insert using a knitting needle or similar to push the wadding right down to the ends. Turn in and stitch closed the open end of the tube.

• Stitch together the three ends and plait the tubes and hand stitch to secure.

• Sew a brass ring onto each end and hang over a wall-mounted hook. The ends can be enhanced with a fabric rosette in the three colours.

Pelmets and valances

Pelmets and valances give definition to a window, making the most of an interesting shape, and adding something special to a dull window. Valances are usually made of the same fabric as the curtain, folded into soft pleats. They can be made using curtain heading tape in pleats or deep gathers and attached by hooks to a pelmet board or track. The shape too can vary to add interest.

Pelmets, which are rigid and can even be made from plywood, are more economical with fabric than valances, and will show off an interesting or fussy fabric to very good effect. They can be used with a blind as well as curtains, and can be cut to any shape that takes your fancy.

The same rules apply as for tiebacks. As long as the proportions are right, anything goes. A pelmet or valance should always be deep enough, so that it does not look mean or ridiculous. The usual depth of a pelmet or valance is one fifth the total depth of the curtain. Always make a template, especially with a pelmet, and try it out in position to make sure your pelmet or valance is deep enough. Both pelmets and softer valances benefit from an edge defined with fringing, piping, a bias strip, cord or even tassels.

MAKING A PELMET BOARD

The pelmet board is really a shelf measuring about 10cm wide, and made from plywood of 1.5-2cm thickness. Make sure the pelmet board is wide enough to overlap each side of the curtain track by at least 5cm. Fix it 6-8cm above the window. The board need not be square – a D-shaped pelmet board looks very stylish on fixed headed curtains or pelmets. A piece of curtain track is bent slightly and fixed to the underside of the pelmet board.

Before fixing the pelmet board to the wall, nail two pieces of plywood, each 10cm square, to each end to make returns. Screw angle brackets to the underside of the board at each end and at 30cm intervals along the board. Screw the angle brackets to the wall and so attach the pelmet board. An additional piece of plywood attached to the front of the pelmet board will give it extra definition and strength, and can be painted or used for stapling fabric straight onto the board (see page 37).

When measuring up for your pelmet, allow for the returns (the piece between the front of the pelmet and the wall) and make sure the pelmet will be deep enough to be in proportion with the curtain.

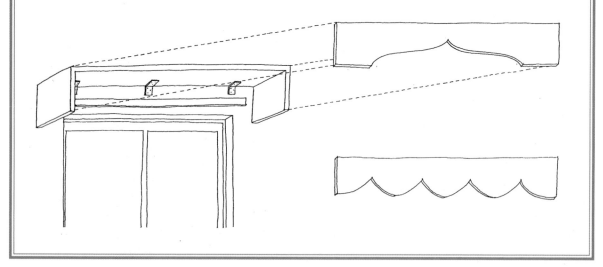

Box pelmets

Whilst soft pelmets are made in much the same way as curtains, using heading tape which then hooks onto pelmet track, a box pelmet is simpler to make and can look very stylish. Measure the pelmet board, including the return boards, and cut out a piece of main fabric and a piece of lining to that size and shape, adding 1.5cm for turnings on all sides (hide any seams by positioning them on the returns). Cut a piece of pelmet stiffener to the finished size of the pelmet, without turnings.

Press the main fabric and place right side down. Remove the backing from one side of the stiffener and press the exposed side centrally onto the main fabric. Remove the backing from the other side of the stiffener. Fold the edges of the main fabric over the stiffener, clipping if necessary, and press into place.

Press the lining, turn over 1.5cm around the edges to the wrong side, and press. Position the lining over the stiffener, press down and smooth into place. Slipstitch the edges of the lining to the edges of the main fabric. Fold enough fabric at each end of the pelmet strip to cover the returns, and crease well.

To fix the pelmet to the pelmet board, use touch and close tape attached to the edge of the board and the back of the pelmet, or pin with drawing pins (cover the pins with braid or trimming attached using fabric glue).

Pelmets can be shaped by cutting the fabric, lining and stiffener to a pattern drawn out on a template, or by fixing a shaped piece of plywood to the front of the pelmet board and by painting or stapling fabric onto it. Either method will benefit from braid detail on the edge to define the shape.

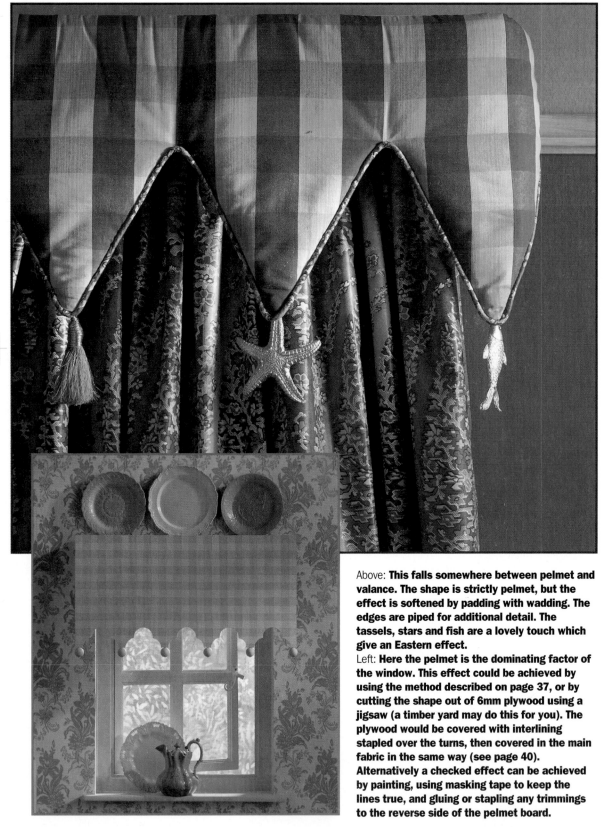

Above: **This falls somewhere between pelmet and valance. The shape is strictly pelmet, but the effect is softened by padding with wadding. The edges are piped for additional detail. The tassels, stars and fish are a lovely touch which give an Eastern effect.**

Left: **Here the pelmet is the dominating factor of the window. This effect could be achieved by using the method described on page 37, or by cutting the shape out of 6mm plywood using a jigsaw (a timber yard may do this for you). The plywood would be covered with interlining stapled over the turns, then covered in the main fabric in the same way (see page 40). Alternatively a checked effect can be achieved by painting, using masking tape to keep the lines true, and gluing or stapling any trimmings to the reverse side of the pelmet board.**

Lambrequins

Lambrequins, very fashionable in the last century, with sides sometimes extending down to the sill, are a particularly elegant way of framing a window. They solve problems such as awkward windows which would be too high for curtains, and add a little flair to a dull view. When used on their own, they are purely ornamental, but here a matching roman blind gives privacy at night and blocks out light when necessary. An ungathered piece of organdie or muslin would look just as effective.

You will need:

- Main fabric
- Wadding
- Lining fabric
- Plywood
- Piping and piping fabric
- Staple gun
- Paper for a template
- A jigsaw

1. Make a template, to the shape required, from stiff paper. Use this template to cut a piece of 6mm plywood, and to cut out your main fabric and wadding, adding seam allowances (if you are covering a pelmet board in a similar way remember to cut returns). If you choose to pipe the edges, cover piping in the same or contrasting fabric, then pin and tack the piping to the right side of the main fabric.

2. Cut a 5cm strip of fabric. This will be used to attach the main fabric at the back of the lambrequin. Lay the main fabric, piping casing and 5cm strip of fabric right sides together, and machine stitch through all three layers at once.

3. Cover the front of the plywood with wadding, sticking it with glue.

4. Lay the fabric face down, with the wadding-covered plywood face down on top of it. Pull the fabric taut so that there are no creases, matching the piping or seam to the edge of the plywood. Fold the 5cm strip of main fabric over to the back of the plywood, fold and mitre to fit, and staple to the reverse side of the plywood, over the wadding.

5. Cut a piece of lining fabric using the original template, and turn in a hem around the edge so that the lining fits just inside the edge of the plywood, covering the edge of the main fabric. Staple the lining to the reverse of the lambrequin, to conceal the raw edges of the fabric and wadding.

1

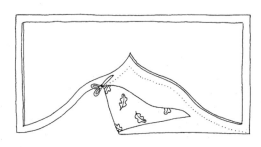

4

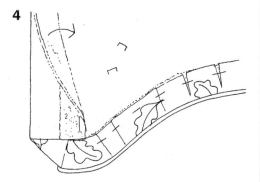

2

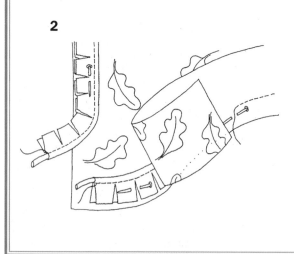

5

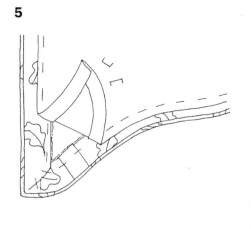

Flounced valances

These soft swathes of fabric are a beautiful way of framing a window, and, for privacy, a simple blind can be positioned behind. Flounced valances provide one of the simplest ways to dress a window. They can drape over a curtain pole in any way you choose, and require very little sewing. Soft fabrics, such as cottons, voile, muslin or silk work best.

To make your own, experiment using an old sheet to find the shape you prefer. Calculate the amount of fabric needed by hanging a piece of cord or string over the pole and down each side of the window to the length required. Position large brass curtain rings at each end of the pole, pull the fabric through one ring, around the pole, then through the other ring to hold it in place, arranging the fabric so that it looks as full as possible.

TIPS

- Line the fabric in a contrasting colour to add interest.
- If the amount of fabric needed is no more than 7m, you could use a silk sari as a pelmet flounce.
- For a more formal look, use a shorter length of fabric, and loop it over decorative hooks set at the top two corners of the window. Fix the fabric in stiffer folds using fabric stiffener.

Tassels and trimmings

Such details can add the finishing touch to a pair of curtains. A silk fringe can make a swagged valance truly elegant, and a bobble edging can make curtains seem wittier and more interesting. From a practical point of view, trims hide joins and cover edges. Trimmings are made from many types of yarn; pure silk and spun rayon have a sheen, chenille is currently fashionable, as are cotton, wool, linen and jute. Include them in your design plans right from the start so they don't look like an afterthought (many companies include co-ordinating trimmings in their sample books).

Tassels, which can be used suspended from poles, or used as tiebacks, come in a huge variety of colours, and some are multicoloured, to draw together the colours in a fabric, blind or pelmet. Small tassels could be hung from each point of a pelmet. Trimmings can also include piping and bias binding, which help to bring out the dominant colour in your decorating scheme, perhaps a hue in the fabric which matches the walls or carpet.

Once again, of course, proportion is very important. Do not let a trimming look like an apology. It must be as much of a statement as the curtains themselves.

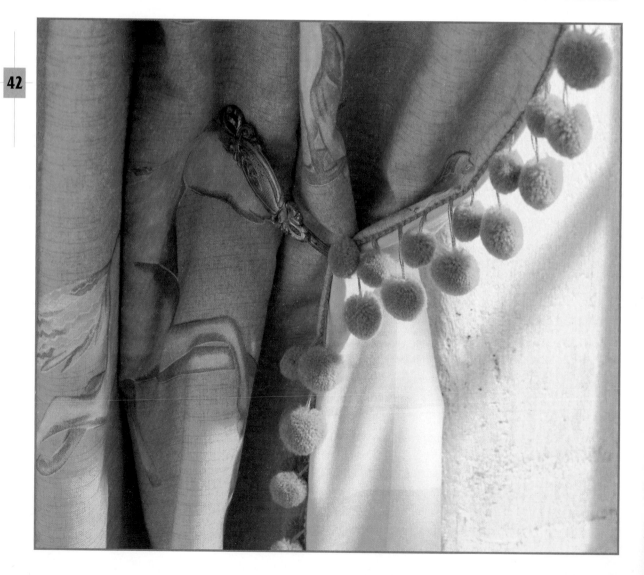

TIPS

- Where there is no room for a pelmet, stencil or paint freehand a design around the edges of the window (above).
- To co-ordinate a bedroom look, add a trim down the edge of plain curtains or a pelmet, using the same fabric as on a bed cover or dressing-table cloth. Alternatively, use patterned curtains and edge the plain bedspread.
- Paint a shaped pelmet board in a plain colour which contrasts with the curtain fabric. This is a good way of toning down a busy fabric pattern.
- If sewing a trim is difficult, use fabric glue.

Left: **Tassels come in a large variety of shapes and sizes. Multi-coloured tassels will help to draw together the colours of your decorating scheme.**

Below: **Some fabric companies include co-ordinated trimmings with their fabric samples. Make sure trimmings are bold enough to make a statement.**

45

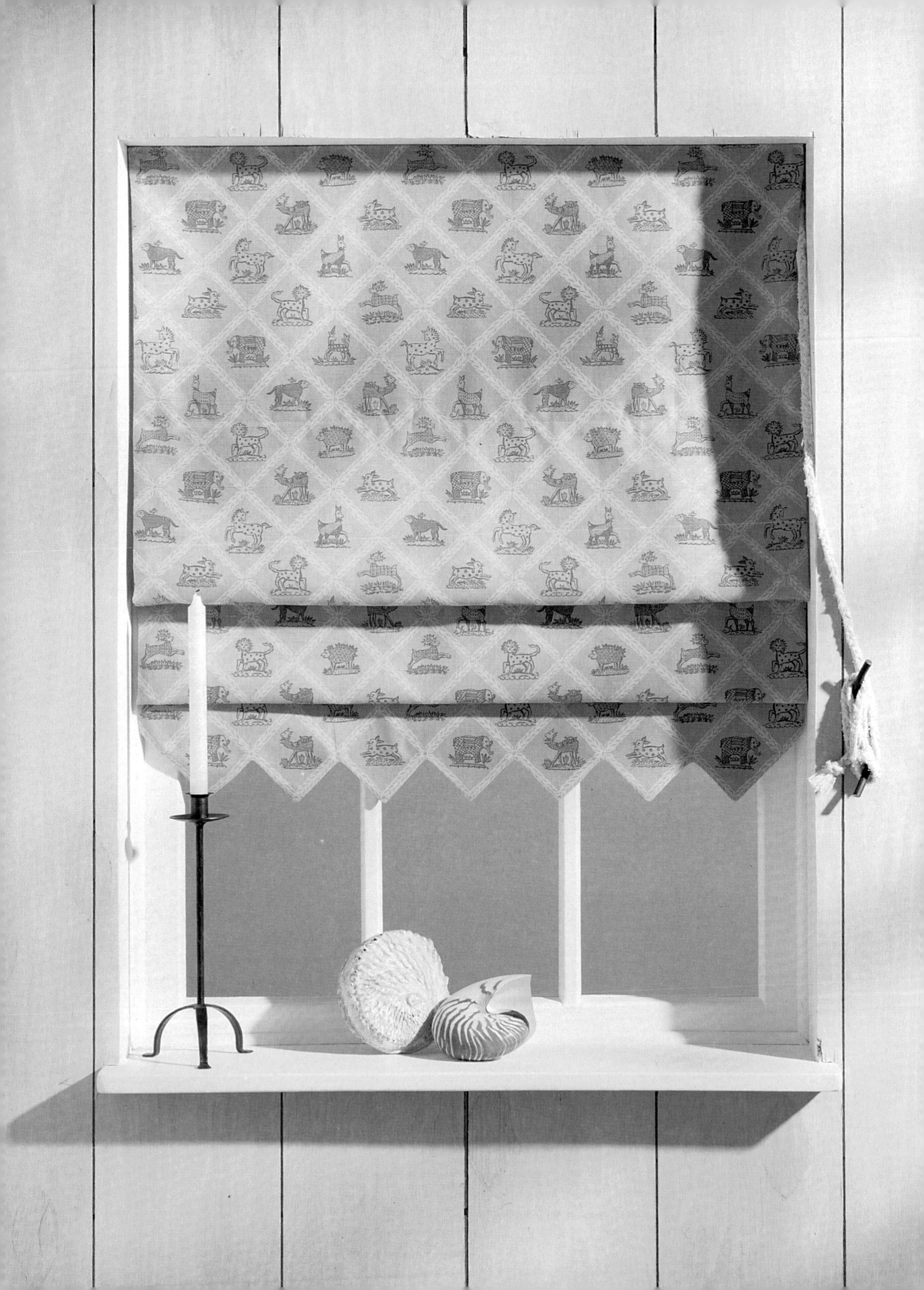

4 Blinds and shutters

Though blinds and shutters serve the same purpose as curtains (to block out light, keep in warmth and maintain privacy), the beauty of them is their versatility. A blind can solve the problem of an awkwardly shaped window in a deep recess. The simple, unfussy lines of blinds can be dressed up or left plain for an uncluttered look; for this reason they work well on small windows which would be overpowered by curtains. Blinds are ideal in a kitchen or bathroom because they can be drawn up out of the way of splashes when not in use. They suit both modern, minimalist decor (shutters are particularly good for this) or more lush surroundings, where festoons would fit the bill, and most of all, blinds use less fabric than curtains, so can be a more economical way to dress your windows. As a result, because Roman and roller blinds are essentially a flat piece of fabric, you can afford to be a little more extravagant in your choice of fabric than you might have been when choosing fabric for curtains.

As with all window dressing, the proportions need careful attention; blinds should ideally be longer than they are wide. Over a very wide window, several blinds will help control light as well as break the monotony of the window itself.

MEASURING UP FOR BLINDS

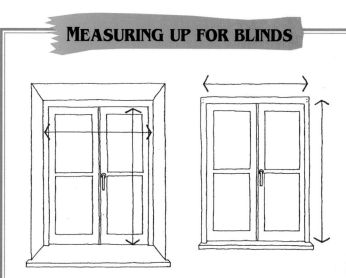

Roller blind
In a recess: measure the width of the top of the window from one side of the recess to the other, and deduct 1.5cm either side for the roller mechanism. Leave 3cm from the top of the recess to allow for the thickness of the rolled up blind, depending on the drop of the window.

Without a recess: position the blind along the top of the window frame or on the wall above the window, though this position will let in more light.

Roman blinds
In a recess: Roman blinds are fixed onto a wooden batten which is itself fixed to the top of the window or to the ceiling of the recess. Measure the drop from the top of the batten to the sill, and the width of the window frame.

Without a recess: the batten can be screwed into the wall above a window, or attached as before to the window frame. Measure the drop as before.

Austrian blinds
In a recess: Austrian blinds sit on a special track. Measure the width of the top of the window frame down to the sill.

Without a recess: allow the track to extend about 7cm both sides of the window, and for length, measure from the top of the track to the sill.

Roller blinds

These are the plainest, most uncomplicated, blinds, which work especially well positioned behind a decorative curtain, even one that is pulled back permanently and held with an extravagant tieback (see Chapter 3). Stiffened close-weave fabrics like cotton are ideal for roller blinds as they keep their shape well and lend themselves to fabric paint if you want to make them a little more decorative. The bottom of a roller blind can also be shaped in an interesting way.

Roller blinds are ideal for filtering out the strong sun of a south facing window. A roller blind made in black-out fabric will help keep summer's early-morning light out of a child's room. To work well as any sort of light filter or excluder, however, the blind is best placed right up against the glass. This means that a roller blind does not work well at a small window which has an arm latch that protrudes when open.

49

You will need:

Fabric, ready stiffened or
  stiffened with fabric spray
Lath
Paper template (optional)
Roller-blind fixing kit
Cord pull
Spirit level
Tacks

1. Fit the roller-blind fixings at the window as outlined on page 47, using a spirit level to make sure they are absolutely aligned, and measure the amount of fabric you will need. Cut the pole to the required length.
2. Ready-stiffened fabric can be cut exactly to size as it will not fray and needs no side turnings. Add 30cm to the length to allow for the casing and to ensure that the pole is still covered when the blind is pulled right down. If you are stiffening your own fabric, follow the manufacturer's instructions on the container, and treat the fabric before cutting as fabric stiffener can cause fabric to shrink.
3. At the base, make a double 4cm hem (8cm in all). Press and stitch across the edge of the hem, and up one side to make a casing for the lath. Cut the lath so it is 2cm shorter than the casing, insert the lath, and stitch the open end closed.
4. Turn 1.5cm down from the top edge to the right side and press down with your fingers.

Place the blind right side up, lay the roller across the top edge of the blind, with the spring mechanism to the left, and fold the top edge of the fabric to meet the guidelines marked on the roller. Use tacks to fix the fabric in place at 2cm intervals along the edge of the roller.
5. Make up the cord pull, knotting one end of the cord through the holder, and threading the opposite end through the acorn. Screw into place in the centre of the lath, on the front of the blind.
6. Roll the blind around the roller, and hang the blind onto the fixed brackets. Pull it down a couple of times to get the tension right.

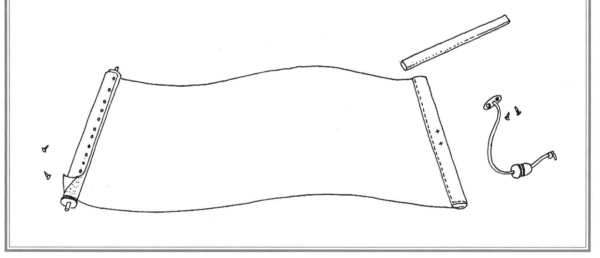

Venetian and vertical louvered blinds

There was a time when no-one would have given these blinds houseroom; they were usually found on the windows of dowdy offices. New materials, however, have made both Venetian and vertical blinds more stylish and quite the rage. Venetian blinds can now be colour co-ordinated, and they are available in plastic, metal, and, perhaps most attractive of all, wood. Vertical blinds, which pivot open and closed, can be made from canvas, wood or even silk.

Both sorts of blinds can be bought ready-made, or made-to-order, which makes them expensive, but they complement a minimalist decor and make the most of a very dull window with a duller aspect. They are difficult to clean, but they have a security bonus as they can be shut very firmly to deter snoopers.

Roman blinds

Of all the styles of blinds, the Roman blind is perhaps the most appealing. A Roman blind covers the window in the same way as a roller blind, but cords or rods attached to the back of the blind mean that when it is pulled up it falls into neat, tailored folds.

It can be lined and interlined for heat efficiency, fitted behind an interesting pelmet or decorative curtain, and, because it is a simple piece of fabric, shows off an interesting fabric design beautifully (cotton prints are most suitable). A Roman blind can fit in a recess or in front of the window, and the edges can be shaped or finished off with interesting trimming to make them even more stylish.

If more than one width of fabric is necessary the fabric can be joined together with flat seams, but it is best to use two or more individual blinds for very wide windows. Making a Roman blind can be daunting for the inexperienced and many prefer to call in the professional. But although it involves a number of steps to make a Roman blind, they are not complicated in themselves.

A Roman blind can be made with either strips of tape with eyes which are threaded with cord, or with dowels sewn into the blind horizontally. The latter gives it a crisper edge once it is pulled up, and needs less arranging to keep its tailored look. The following method uses dowels.

You will need:
Main fabric
Co-ordinating lining fabric
Dowels (8 or 9mm)
Touch and close tape
Batten (5 x 2.5cm piece of timber) and screws
Fabric glue
Tacks
Screw Eyes
Brass or plastic rings
Cleat and blind cord
Acorn
Bradawl

Method:
1. Cut the batten to the width of the window frame, if the blind is to sit in the recess, or as wide as you want if it is to sit above the window.
2. Cut a rectangle of main fabric wide enough and long enough to wrap around the cut batten without too much excess fabric at the back. Spread fabric glue over the batten, and carefully wrap the fabric around it, trimming off any excess fabric. Secure the fabric neatly at the back of the batten with a few tacks. Allow to dry completely.
3. Using the bradawl, make a hole at each end of the base of the batten and attach screw eyes through which the blind cord will be run. Put one in the middle too if the blind is very wide. Fix the screw eyes into the holes, being careful not to tear the fabric. Glue a length of touch and close tape along the front of the batten and fix tacks in two or three places to keep it secure.
4. Fix the batten to the window frame or wall with screws (and wall plugs if into masonry). Make sure that the screws are long enough to pass through the batten and then into the wall for at least 2cm.
5. Cut the main fabric as wide as the batten length, plus 6cm for the side turnings, and as long as the window height, plus 6cm for hem and heading.
6. Cut the required amount of lining. The lining will need to be longer than the main fabric to allow for the casings of the dowels. Each casing will need 7.5cm of

fabric, and there should be dowels every 20cm down the blind leaving 10cm between the bottom dowel and the bottom edge of the blind. Calculate how many dowels (and therefore dowel casings) you will need and add an 8cm seam allowance and 4cm heading and hem allowance to your final lining measurement.

7. Turn in the sides of the lining in a 2cm double seam (4cm in all) either side and machine stitch close to the fold. Mark out where the dowel casings will be (each casing needing 7.5cm of lining fabric – see step 6), making sure that the seams are absolutely parallel and at right angles to the edge of the fabric.

8. Fold the lining for the dowel casing so that the seams meet. Tack and machine stitch, closing only one end of the dowel casing. Press.

9. Turn in a 3cm hem top and bottom on the main fabric and a 3cm seam on each side and press.

10. Lay the lining, wrong side down, over the back of the blind. Turn under 2cm at the top and bottom, and pin and tack through both the lining and main fabric. Tack just above the dowel casings. Slipstitch along the top, bottom and each side.

11. Machine stitch along the dowel lines through both the lining and main fabric, making sure that the tension is correct. Tack a length of touch and close tape along the back of the blind at the top (so it meets the touch and close tape on the batten and still leaves enough fabric at the top of the blind to cover the batten), and machine stitch into place.

12. Insert the dowels into the casings and hand stitch the end of each casing closed. Sew brass or plastic rings to the dowel pockets, in line with the screw eyes on the batten, including up the centre if necessary.

13. Lay the blind face down. Decide on which side you want the pull cord to hang (on this blind the cord will hang on the left of the window). Cut two pieces of cord measuring twice the length of the blind. Tie one length of cord to the lowest ring on the bottom left of the blind, run it through the rings up the blind. Now tie a length of cord to the ring on the bottom right of the blind, and run up through the rings as before.

14. Press the touch and close tape at the top of the blind onto the strip of tape on the batten, making sure that the blind is straight. Now, lifting up the blind, run the cords through the screw eyes right to left on the batten until they meet on the left-hand side of the blind.

15. Hold the cords taut and pull up the blind, adjusting the folds so that they are straight and neat. Thread the cords through the acorn and tie in the knot, cutting the cords if they are too long, but making sure that you allow enough slack for the blind to hang its full length when it is let down.

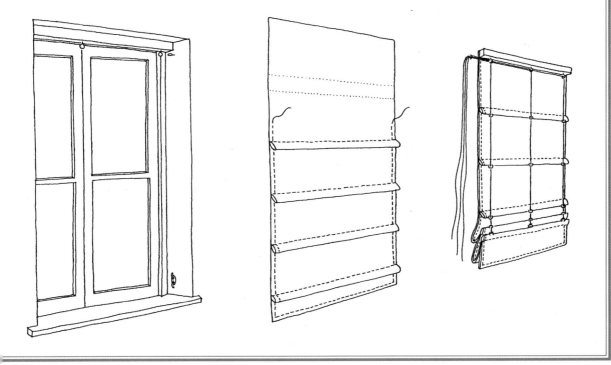

Austrian or festoon blinds

The festoon blind with its full gathers has a romantic, frilly feel about it, which was wildly popular in country houses two centuries ago. Nowadays, this style works well in a bedroom or bathroom and is least suited to a kitchen, where the simplicity of a Roman or roller blind would be more practical. Festoons are a rather fussy solution to a small window, but on a longer window, especially with a trim detail, can look really stunning.

Austrian blinds are made in much the same way as Roman blinds and you may prefer to use a professional blind-making service. Their fullness means that they are less economical with fabric.

54

An Austrian blind hangs here behind a simple lambrequin decorated with rosettes, which helps to tone down the fussiness of the blind.

You will need:

- Main fabric
- Lining
- Heading tape
- Weights
- Fringe and braid (optional)
- Blind cord
- Cleat
- Austrian blind track

1. Fix the Austrian blind track into position on the window.

2. Cut your main fabric and lining. The flat, unpleated width should be twice the finished width, plus 8cm for turnings. Add 20cm to the drop for hem and heading.

3 If necessary, join the widths of main fabric and lining using flat seams. Press.

4. Place the main fabric and the lining wrong sides together, and turn in a double seam (4cm in all) down each side of the blind. Tack and stitch.

5. On the wrong side of the blind pin the two outer rows of looped tapes into position, placing them vertically 10cm in from the hemmed side edge and 3cm up from the bottom edge. Then position the two inner tapes equally between the two outer ones (at about 30cm intervals, depending on the width of the blind). Make sure all the loops match up horizontally, then pin, tack and stitch the tapes into place.

6. Stitch weights into lining bags at each corner of the blind and at the base of each tape, then turn up a double hem (5cm in all) at the base of the blind. Tack and herringbone stitch. Hand stitch the fringe or braid onto the bottom of the blind.

7. Turn over a double hem (5cm in all) at the top of the blind, catching the top of the looped tapes. Pin and tack a strip of heading onto the top edge of the blind, knotting the cords at one end and keeping the cords at the other end free. Machine stitch into place.

8. Follow step 12 of the Roman blind instructions for threading the cord up the looped tape, starting on the left and repeating with each row of tape. Pull the cords of the heading tape until the blind is gathered to the required width and secure the cords with a bow or cord tidy. Fit the gathered tape with the same number of curtain hooks as you have screw eyes on the track and hang the blind. Loop the cords that run up the tapes through the screw eyes on the track until all the cords are hanging together at the cleat side of the window.

9. With the curtain down and with equal tension in all the cords, pull up the blind until it hangs straight, feed the cords through the acorn, knot and trim the cords to a practical length. Fix the cleat and wind the cord around it.

NOTE: A tassel attached to the bottom of the cords in place of an acorn adds interesting detail.

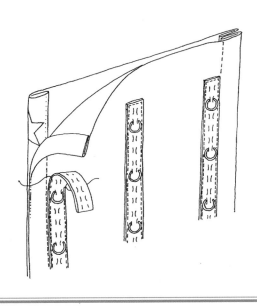
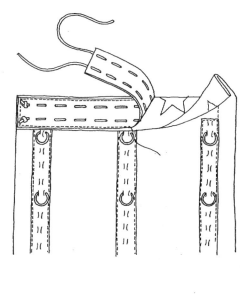

These reverse roller blinds are made from canvas which is tough and hard wearing (though they are best left in one position, rather than rolled up and down frequently). Cut the canvas to fit the window, and two lengths of thick wooden dowel slightly wider than the width of the canvas. Lay out the canvas right side up and place a length of dowel on top. Roll the canvas around the dowel until the edge of the canvas is in a straight line across the dowel. Fix with tacks every 2cm. Repeat at the bottom of the blind. Attach the blind to the window by screwing cuphooks large enough to support the dowel into the top corners of the architrave. Roll the blind as high as you want it, and secure with a length of rope looped around the top dowel and knotted loosely around the bottom one.

Cheat's blinds

There are many ways to make appealing blinds without the fuss of making the more complicated versions.

• A loosely woven cloth or very fine raffia fabric will filter strong sunlight in a south facing room and create something more stylish than a net curtain. Cut two lengths of bamboo (available from garden centres) slightly wider than the window. Cut a length of cloth or raffia, painting the edges of the latter with clear glue to stop them fraying, stitch a narrow casing hem top and bottom and push the bamboo through each casing. Hook the bamboo over cup hooks screwed into the architrave.

• A beautiful piece of lace, such as broderie anglaise, hung half-way down a bathroom window to give privacy, looks beautiful with light shining though it. Equally effective would be a piece of fabric stencilled with a simple design using fabric paint. Fix it to a thin brass pole using brass café-curtain hooks.

• A bead curtain or blind catches the light and makes an appealing sound as it moves. To make a bead curtain, use strong nylon thread and vary the colours and shapes of the beads that you choose. Fix a batten across the doorway, and tie the nylon thread firmly to screw eyes fixed into the batten.

Shutters

Traditional Georgian/Victorian shutters fold back neatly into recesses at both sides of the window, but shutters can work just as well fitted to windows with no recess at all. They bend back out of the way when light and a view is required, and can be pulled over to shield the room from sunlight, or provide security and a measure of sound proofing. The unfussy lines of louvered shutters mean they look just as good with a simple decor as with a busy scheme. Equally, a cotton flounced valance, with its soft lines, makes an interesting contrast to the straight lines of half shutters **(below left)**.

Shutters need not be restricted to windows. Hanging full length, they are a good means of covering French doors, and, because of their design, would work well set on the outside of the door, if treated with the correct exterior fluid or paint for protection. By the very nature of their fit, shutters usually have to be made to measure, which means that they are not cheap, but they will usually outlive curtains or blinds.

57

5 Fabrics and basic techniques

Fabrics

There are really no hard and fast rules for which fabrics are most suitable for curtains and blinds. As explained in Chapter 1, you will have been guided in the right direction by the practical requirements of the window and room in question. After that it is a question of finding an appealing fabric which has the right weight, pattern or sheen, and is easy to work with.

When you have chosen your fabric, make a note of its composition, the preferred method of cleaning (see page 63) and its ability to withstand fading and shrinking. Always buy enough fabric, as fabric from another roll is unlikely to match exactly.

Batik cotton fabric with interesting patterns made using a wax-resist technique originating in the Far East.

Brocade heavy, traditional fabric (woven on a Jacquard loom) now made from man-made fibres, with a raised design, often of flowers. Ideal for formal curtains.

Broderie anglaise pretty cotton or linen fabric with flower or leaf design in open embroidery. Ideal for thin curtains or single-thickness blinds, and for edging accessories in a child's room.

Butter muslin inexpensive, thin material ideal for dyeing. However, it does shrink and crease badly.

Calico thick cream cotton, useful in its original form or when painted or stencilled.

Chintz a glazed cotton (the resin is dust repellent) which originated in India and is usually patterned with large-scale flowers and bird designs. Plain chintz is used for piping or banding. Chintz has a traditional country-house feel about it, though it can be at home anywhere. Unfortunately cleaning will dull the glaze, which will need to be reapplied.

Cotton the most useful curtain or blind fabric, often blended with man-made fibres to give strength and make cleaning easier. Available in a wide variety of weights, colours and prints.

Crewelwork wool embroidery often in chain stitch, frequently on cream-coloured, loosely woven Indian fabric. The embroidered fabric makes attractive curtains but the colours vary considerably from roll to roll.

Cretonne hard wearing cotton fabric similar to unglazed chintz. It is washable and easy to care for.

Damask luscious self-patterned traditional cotton or silk fabric woven like brocade on a Jacquard loom, but flatter than brocade and reversible, with more depth than flat cottons.

Gingham fresh cotton fabric printed in squares of colour on white, or stripes, available in a variety of weights. It works well in kitchens or children's rooms, and mixes effectively with floral patterns.

Interlining bleached or unbleached blanket-type fabric available in a variety of thicknesses. Synthetic versions are the cheapest but they are less good for draught exclusion or for softness. Domette is the best choice of interlining for blinds, as it is thinner.

Lace delicate open-work fabric, usually made from cotton, available in an endless variety of patterns. More stylish than net for privacy or light filtering, it is also useful for trimming details.

Madras cotton checked or striped cotton fabric imported from India, inexpensive but prone to shrinking.

Moiré silk or cotton fabric with watermark effect, luxurious looking but ruined by water spills.

Sateen blended fabric (usually including cotton), which is soft with a shiny finish. Most often used as lining, it is also useful for curtains.

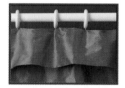

Satin expensive looking fabric with a sheen on one side, available in a variety of strong jewel-like colours giving lots of scope for colour schemes.

Silk natural fabric available in a variety of weaves, from the softest to shot silk (shantung), which is unevenly textured wild silk. Silk is an expensive choice for cur-

taining, and difficult to care for, but the wide choice of deep colours may make it a worthwhile investment.

Ticking hard-wearing sturdy cotton fabric, traditionally used for covering mattresses. Now available in a wide variety of colours, it is inexpensive, and useful for fresh looking modern furnishings.

Toile de Jouy cotton or linen fabric (originally from Jouy, France), printed with scenes of pastoral life on a cream background. Though currently fashionable, it can be overpowering.

Velvet fabric (often cotton, but can be silk, nylon, etc.) with thick lush pile. Though difficult to care for, velvet makes wonderful curtains, which are very effective draught excluders.

Voile sheer cotton best used as thin curtaining, or as a blind behind a fixed pelmet or lambrequin.

Wadding fluffy man-made fibre used to add plumpness to goblet headings and pleated tiebacks.

Tracks

It is a good idea to look at the type of tracks available before you decide on the style of curtain you will make. The choice is very wide: tracks with pelmets attached, tracks that overlap where the curtains meet, tracks which can be covered with fabric show when the curtain is pulled back. There are even double tracks for hanging sheer curtains behind thicker ones. Tracks with pull cords are perhaps the most useful because they avoid the need to touch the curtains which therefore stay clean for longer. There are also tracks for blinds, and tracks specifically designed for bow and bay windows, making the job of dressing them infinitely easier.

• Seek out a specialist curtain shop for advice. Though large D.I.Y stores stock a good range, their salespeople are less likely to be knowledgeable.

• Make sure the track is strong enough to support the weight of your finished curtains.

• Check that the fixings are of good quality and that you have the correct size of screw and wall plug if drilling into plaster or brick.

- Uncorded track can be cut to fit the window exactly.
- Make sure that you are well clear of pipes and electricity wires before you start drilling into the wall around a window.
- Track should be the width of the window plus an extra amount to allow the curtain to be pulled back, and should be positioned 8-12 cm above the window. Fix the brackets at each end of the track and at 30cm intervals along the length of the track.
- Use extended brackets to make a long curtain stand away from radiators or proud of a recess.

Poles

Curtain poles provide an additional decorative aspect, given the variety of finials, colours and widths on offer. They can be left plain, or swathed in fabric to make an impromptu pelmet. Wooden poles are more common and economical and, for this reason, it may be necessary to pay a little more than normal for something slightly more unusual. Alternatively, buy a cheap pole, and paint it, including the rings and finial, with wood stain to co-ordinate with the curtain. Gilded finials look very stylish. If you feel inspired you might want to cut out your own shapes in thick fibre board.

Brass poles have always been popular. Steel and iron poles are now also tremendously fashionable. They vary in quality and price, but can add a simplicity which suits an uncluttered cottage-style decor.

- A pole can be anything from 2.5cm to 8cm thick. Make sure it is strong enough to support your curtains without putting too much strain on the fixings.
- Make sure that the pole is in proportion to your curtain heading.
- When buying a wooden pole, make sure it is completely straight and not warped.
- When fixing poles to the wall, the brackets should be several centimetres in from the finials.
- If the pole is being fitted into a recess and there is no room for finials, fit the pole ends into pole sockets.

A sewing machine and the following basic stitching techniques are all you need to start making your first pair of curtains.

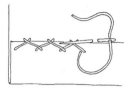

Herringbone stitch is used to hem heavy curtains, to join interlining and wadding and to attach non-fusible interfacing. Work from left to right, with the wrong side of fabric towards you. Bring the needle up through the hem taking a short stitch, move the needle up to the right diagonally and take another short stitch (inserting the needle right to left) just above the hem. Move the needle down to the right diagonally and take another short stitch in the hem (right to left), and so on. The effect will be crossed stitches. Keep the thread fairly loose throughout.

Locking stitch joins together the main fabric and lining in curtains. It is not always necessary but will stop the lining sagging and may improve the hang of curtains made from heavy fabrics. Lay the ready hemmed, seamed curtain fabric and lining wrong sides together. Make sure that the layers are perfectly flat, pin them together from top to bottom in parallel lines, one-third and two-thirds of the way across. Fold the lining back to the first pinned line, and pick up a few threads of the main fabric and then the lining to make a loose horizontal stitch. Bring the thread down the fold, keeping it loose, and make another stitch, continuing in the same way every 5cm or so to the bottom of the lining, thus producing loops of thread. Repeat down the second line.

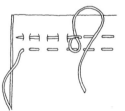

Running stitch is used for gathering hand-sewn curtain headings. Work from right to left, and begin with a backstitch to start off and hold the thread securely, then continue making small, evenly spaced stitches along the fabric. Finish with another backstitch. For gathering, work a second row of stitches 5mm below the first but leave long thread ends as you finish each row.

Gently slide the fabric along the threads until the gather is the required width. Fasten off the loose ends – one method is to wind them in a figure of eight shape around a pin stuck into the end of the gather.

Slipstitch is a virtually invisible stitch, this will hold together folded hems and seams. Working from right to left, catch a few threads of the flat fabric and a few threads of the folded hem fabric in almost the same place, and pull the needle through leaving the thread fairly loose. Repeat along the hem.

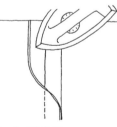

Basic Flat Seam
Place the fabric right sides together, aligning the raw edges. Pin, tack and machine stitch 1.5cm in from the edge, making a few stitches in reverse at each end to keep the seam secure. Make sure the tension of the stitches is not too tight. Open the finished seam and press

flat. Seams may need to be trimmed and/or clipped if they are bulky. Seams that curve should be clipped or notched.

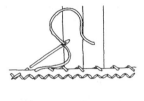

Hems on very heavy fabric should be turned over only once, and may need oversewing, zigzagging or binding to prevent fraying. Hem by hand. On lighter fabrics, especially sheer ones, fold over half the hem allowance, then fold the same amount again. Machine stitch or hem by hand.

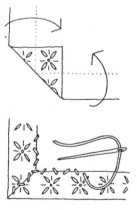

Mitred corners make the fabric less bulky. Turn in the seam, fold the hem, press and then unfold. Fold across the corner, making a triangle, then fold back the seam and hem to form the mitre. Slipstitch in place.